GW00671447

HALLMARKS
AND
DATE LETTERS

on

silver, gold and platinum

N.A.G. PRESS LTD
COLCHESTER, ESSEX

First published 1944
Completely revised 1970
Revised 1977
Reprinted many times

ISBN 7198 0072 2

Printed and bound in Great Britain by
Anchor Brendon Ltd, Tiptree, Essex

INTRODUCTION

This small book first appeared in 1944 and was reprinted many times with minor changes until it was completely revised and re-written in 1970. In the following years several substantial changes occurred such as the incorporation of platinum in the Hallmarking laws, the setting up of the British Hallmarking Council, and the Introduction of an international Hallmark. The opportunity was therefore taken of bringing the book completely up to date, even to include the additional Silver Jubilee mark that could be applied at the beginning of 1977.

The original compiler, Arthur Tremayne, saw the public interest in an easy introduction to a subject which is so vast that some enthusiasts have spent much of their lives exploring it.

Although silver bullion prices have risen rapidly and the prices of antique plate very much more so, which would seem to limit the activity of collectors, public interest in silver and Hallmarking has increased considerably. The result has been much greater attention to lower priced and more readily available Victorian and even later silver.

It is not only old plate that attracts the interest in Hallmarks. Gold jewellery may be marked with the quality, providing invaluable information when assessing its worth. When buying any modern gold or silver, the customer should always check the Hallmark to make sure that the article is made of what it is claimed to be made of.

The term " plate ", still used by the silver trade, has been debased since the invention of electro-plate. Although it properly refers to articles of sterling silver, it has been avoided in this book where it might be ambiguous.

Mr. John Forbes, Deputy Warden of the Worshipful Company of Goldsmiths, and Master of the London Assay Office, freely gave much of his time and deep knowledge of the subject to comb the manuscript for errors and ambiguities and to make valuable suggestions. Mr. A. H. Westwood, the Birmingham Assay Master, now retired, also willingly placed his exceptionally wide experience at my disposal.

ERIC BRUTON

London, 1977

CONTENTS

HISTORY OF ASSAYING

Hallmarking of gold and silver is one of the earliest forms of consumer protection. A standard for silver wares was instituted in the City of London as long ago as the year 1238, under a Royal Ordinance which also commanded the Mayor and Aldermen to select six " discreet goldsmiths " of the City to superintend the craft.

In the year 1300, during the reign of King Edward I, a statute extended the silver standard to the whole of England and anywhere else in the King's domain. It also stated that silver wares had to be tested by the Wardens of the Goldsmiths Guild. If they passed the test, they were stamped with a punch showing a leopard's head. Those that failed to pass were forfeit to the King.

The statute laid down the standard fineness for gold as " the touch of Paris ", and the standard fineness of silver as the same as that of money, known as the sterling standard.

The statute also required the Wardens to go from shop to shop among the workers to assay their gold. Any gold that did not pass was forfeit to the King.

It laid down that all the " good towns of England " where there were goldsmiths should make the same statutes as those of London and that one man should go from each town to London " to seek their sure touch ". This meant that the London standard was to be that for the whole country. Later legislation provided for the marking of gold articles as in the case of silver.

On March 30th, 1327, London goldsmiths received a Royal Charter, forming them into the Worshipful Company of Goldsmiths and giving them powers to enforce the assay and hallmarking laws. The word " Hallmark " is derived from Goldsmiths Hall, the headquarters of the Company.

The " touch " referred to the earliest system of assaying gold. The method was to rub the article being assayed on a " touch stone ", a natural hard black stone. The streaks it made were compared with streaks from a needle of standard gold. Silver, however, appears to have been assayed from an early date by a more accurate method known as " cupellation ".

The cupellation assay was later extended to gold and the methods used have developed and become more and more accurate until today a modern Assay Office has very sophisticated techniques at its disposal.

Scrapings, known as " diet ", are taken from the various component parts of every article and submitted to accurate analysis (assay). If they do not fall below the quality standard, the article is passed for marking. Each office also keeps a " diet box " in which

Goldsmiths Hall, Foster Lane, London, E.C.2, which gave Hallmarking its name.

is kept a proportion of scrapings from articles that have passed assay. These scrapings are also periodically checked to see that standards are being preserved.

There are at present four Assay Offices operating in Great Britain—at London, Birmingham, Sheffield, and Edinburgh. Formerly, there were eleven, including one in Ireland, but over the years six have been closed. The Dublin Assay Office is still active. In earlier times a number of minor Guilds also marked their wares locally.

THE HALLMARK

A Hallmark is a stamp applied to an article of precious metal after test by assay, by an official Assay Office, to denote fineness of quality. At the present time two qualities of silver and four qualities of gold are marked.

No article or part of an article is marked unless it is first assayed and found to be of the standard of quality required by law. Although the assaying and marking authorities are not government officials, they operate under full legal powers.

The British Hallmark is of unquestioned and unquestionable integrity as a guarantee of quality. It is accepted as such in every part of the world.

Until as recently as 1773, the punishment for counterfeiting the Hallmark was death. It was then changed to 14 years' transportation to a penal colony. Now the maximum penalty is 10 years' imprisonment.

A complete Hallmark consists of four punch marks and looks like this one on silver:

Makers' mark	Standard mark	Assay Office mark	Date letter

or this one on gold:

Makers' mark	Standard mark	Assay Office mark	Date letter

The marks are known by the names shown above them. Strictly speaking, the first mark is the " Maker's Mark ", and the other three are the " Hall's Marks ". For convenience, however, the whole set is known as the " Hallmark ".

Hallmarks are usually, but not always, punched in a row with the maker's mark at one end or the other. The size of a Hallmark may be very small so that a magnifying glass is needed to read it or it may be nearly as big, say, as a finger-tip.

Which punches are chosen depend on the size of the article and the maker's wishes.

Some articles bear several Hallmarks because they were made of several parts which have to be assayed and marked separately. A silver pot with a hinged lid is an example. The four punches are:

1. MAKER's MARK, impressed by the maker before sending the articles to the Hall. Nowadays it always consists of the initials of the man or firm responsible for making the piece or causing it to be made. A shaped punch, of which initials are the main feature of the design, is permissible.

The mark need not represent the actual maker; indeed in 1973 it was renamed the SPONSOR'S MARK. It may represent the name of another manufacturer, a wholesaler, or a retailer. Its main purpose is to identify the person responsible for manufacturing the piece. Thus any trader may register a punch at Goldsmiths Hall or other Assay Office, and send or cause to be sent, articles for assay and marking.

The early maker's mark consisted of a symbol, which was permitted up to 1695. Later, initials were used either with or without the symbol. On Britannia silver the mark was the first two letters of the maker's surname.

The modern system is to use the initials of an individual, the partners of a firm, or a company. The initials are usually surrounded by a shield and the Assay Office will only accept a design of the maker's mark if it is distinct from that or any other mark registered at that Office.

2. ASSAY OFFICE MARK, also known as the " Town Mark ". This identifies the office at which the assaying and marking were done.

3. STANDARD MARK. This guarantees that the quality of the metal is not below the legal standard indicated by the mark. The quality may be above that indicated.

All refiners and bullion dealers sell gold and silver that " reports " a little higher than the standard it is stated to be. The reason is that it is impossible to alloy gold or silver to an exact standard. If a maker submits an article for assay, he wants to be sure that the metal and the solder he uses are up to standard.

Rejection of the article by an Assay Office can be expensive, because the Office will " batter " the article—probably in a press— before returning it, so that it cannot be sold or even repaired.

4. DATE LETTER, a letter of the alphabet to denote the year in which the article was stamped. It is changed annually and is of a character which, in combination with a series of shields of special design, will give a wide variety of letters to avoid duplication.

A separate date letter symbol was first used in London in 1478. The practice of the London Office has always been to use a definite series of cycles, each of 20 letters, but at first in provincial offices much freedom of choice was displayed in both the length of the cycles, and the consistent use of the style of character.

Between 1773 and 1823–4 Sheffield even altered the sequences of letters and from 1780 to 1843 sometimes used a crown in the letter punch. The date on which Birmingham and Sheffield changed their date letter is regulated by statute. The other Offices changed their date letters annually on a date to suit their own arrangements, mainly following tradition. Each Office now has the same series of letters.

In the lists of date letters on pages 29 to 40, some of the very earliest have been omitted since it is highly unlikely that anyone will find silver of such early date.

In view of the fact that silver articles dated before 1700 are exceptionally rare and valuable, it is suggested that the date letter for early examples should not be regarded as the sole indication of age. The other markings, as well as the general style of design and workmanship, obvious to an expert, should be taken into consideration.

In the illustrations of the date letters on pages 29 to 40 printer's types to the nearest founts of the punches have been used, except where no type-face approximated the characters used for some of the early cycles.

The punches used by all Assay Offices at the present day are accurately cut from master dies. All the punches used in a series of sizes, and all the duplicate punches, are perfect reproductions of the original dies.

When all punches were hand-cut in the old days, there were occasionally slight differences in style and size, and often of outline and shapes of shields, to be found in letters of the same year. One of these letters illustrated as the date letter of the year should be taken only as a guide.

The date letter was changed annually at the following times:

London	Middle of May
Birmingham	July 1st
Sheffield	End of July
Edinburgh	Second or third week of October
Dublin	January 1st

On January 1st, 1975, all offices came into line with their date letters and restarted with capital A.

THE ASSAY OFFICE OR TOWN MARKS

LONDON. The mark of London is the Leopard's Head. It is known to have been in use since its establishment by statute in 1300. In a later legal reference it is called the "King's Mark", probably because it was taken from the royal arms.

It has been suggested that it should be a Lion's Head and that the error arose through a misunderstanding of the Old French legal term of the early descriptions.

In the earliest marks dating from 1300, the head was uncrowned. The crowned head appeared first in 1478. Various forms of crowned heads followed. The actual form was probably dependent on the skill and fancy of the punch cutter.

The Leopard's Head was not used on silver during the Britannia silver period (1697 to 1720) but it reappeared when sterling was again stamped.

The crown disappeared from the leopard in the mark after 1820–1 and has not been used since.

Although the Leopard's Head is now exclusively the mark used to denote London, it was not always so. Certain provincial Assay Offices used in the early days all the London marks with an additional punch to indicate their own town; they were Chester, Exeter, Newcastle and York.

Although the statute of 1300 gave London goldsmiths certain powers over the rest of the country, this did not prevent provincial goldsmiths from marking their own wares. The provincial Assay Offices were administered by the local guilds of goldsmiths. Their assayers were sworn in before the mayors. The mark was generally based on the arms of the town.

 BIRMINGHAM. The year 1772 was a red-letter date in the annals of the goldsmiths and silversmiths of both Birmingham and Sheffield. It was the year in which an Act of Parliament permitted the establishment of an Assay Office in each city.

The metal trades were in operation in Birmingham as long ago as the 14th century and in the 18th century, Matthew Boulton gave them a new lease of life by devising new methods of manufacture and organisation. His factory at Soho Hill, Handsworth, was one of the show-places of the Midlands.

Boulton was turning out articles in silver and gold in considerable quantities for those days, but was hampered by difficulties of transport and the time taken in sending his wares to Chester to be assayed and marked.

He wanted Birmingham to have its own office and, with the help of the local landowners who wished to promote local industry, he decided on a petition to Parliament.

The matter became public in 1772 and the Sheffield manufacturers also wanting their own Assay Office wrote to Boulton and his partner Fothergill, requesting permission to join in the petition.

The Goldsmiths' Company of London put forward to Parliament a counter petition. The arguments were heard by two special Committees of the House of Commons and witnesses were produced by both sides. Finally, a Bill was passed by the Commons and received the Royal Assent on May 28th, 1773. The next day Mr. Boulton arrived home in triumph to the tune of the ringing bells of Handsworth Church.

The Act gave Birmingham power to assay and mark only silver wares, but in 1824 it was granted power to assay gold wares in addition.

The town mark of Birmingham is an Anchor. The shape has remained quite consistent over the years, although the shape of the shield around it has been changed.

SHEFFIELD. The story of how, in 1773, Sheffield gained the right to assay and mark silver is told in the previous paragraphs about Birmingham.

In 1904, Sheffield was granted power to assay gold wares also. The town mark of Sheffield is a Crown for silver wares. Because much of the Parliamentary business in connection with the Assay Bill was transacted in the Crown and Anchor Tavern in the Strand, London, a place frequented by politicians, it was conjectured by Mr. A. E. Westwood, former Birmingham Assay Master, that Boulton and his Sheffield friends may have taken the two emblems of the tavern's sign as " local marks " for the Sheffield and Birmingham Assay Offices.

From 1780 to 1853, Sheffield also used a small single punch showing the Crown and the date letter. It was applied to small articles instead of the separate town mark and date letter punches.

The quality mark for gold of 18 carat and 22 carat includes a Crown, which would make Sheffield's town mark confusing on wares of these finenesses. For all British gold ware, therefore, the Sheffield Office had another punch representing a York Rose.

From 1975, Sheffield adopted the York Rose as its Town Mark for silver and platinum as well as for gold.

EDINBURGH. In Scotland, methods of assay and marking silver and gold for fineness developed quite independently of those in England. A statute of 1457, in King James II's reign, appointed " a cunning man of gude conscience quhick " to be a " Deacon of the Craft " in each town where goldsmiths worked. The Deacon set his mark with the goldsmith's mark on work brought to him which was of standard fineness.

In places where a goldsmith worked on his own, he took his work to the town officials who put a town mark on it, if it were of standard fineness.

Another statute, of 1485, in James III's reign, provided for a town mark as well as a Deacon's mark. Also in 1485, the Town Council of Edinburgh granted certain privileges to " the Hammermen ", as the guild of hammer-wielding craftsmen was called.

The town mark of Edinburgh is a Castle with Three Embattled Towers on a Rock. It is taken from the city arms and has been used continuously since 1485.

A Goldsmiths' Guild was established in Edinburgh in 1525 whose minutes and records have been carefully preserved, forming a most valuable historical record.

In 1555, in the reign of Queen Mary (Mary, Queen of Scots) it was ordained that no goldsmith should make or sell, either of his own or any other make, silver of the fineness of less than 11 pennyweight in the pound Troy (just under sterling) or gold of less than 22 ct. under pain of death and confiscation of all his moveable goods. In 1586, James VI granted the Deacon and Master of the Goldsmith's Craft at Edinburgh their first letters patent and when it was notified the following year, Edinburgh goldsmiths had the right to search, seize and supervise the craft throughout Scotland. This also separated goldsmiths from other hammermen.

In 1720, the standard for silver in Scotland was raised to the sterling standard as in England.

Edinburgh supervised all the trade in Scotland until the Glasgow Assay Office was established in 1819 by statute. The Glasgow Office was closed in 1964 and now the Edinburgh Office is the only one in Scotland.

 DUBLIN. The Irish craftsmen of the 9th and 10th centuries produced work unsurpassed by any in Europe. Alas, little of the goldsmiths' work remains, but little as there is, it is sufficient to arouse wonder at the freedom and originality of their art in the minds of the modern craftsmen.

There are the well known pre-Gothic examples of the Ardagh Chalice, the Tara Brooch and the Shrine of the Bell of St. Patrick. All three, appropriately enough, are now in the care of the National Museum, Dublin.

With this tradition of invention and accomplishment behind them it is no surprise to learn that the records of Irish goldsmiths go back to the 13th century and a Guild was definitely mentioned in 1498. The Dublin Goldsmiths' Charter was accidentally burnt in 1555 and the City Corporation was asked to replace it. This, also, was near destruction by fire in more recent days.

The goldsmiths were incorporated by Royal Charter of Charles I in 1637. Premises they occupied are known to have been a building in Ormonds Gate. A new Hall was built in Werburgh Place in 1708. Later, the Assay Office was established in the basement of the Custom House. The Office is now in Lower Castle Yard.

During the War of Independence, the Custom House was the scene of a sharp engagement on April 21st, 1921. One of the results was the destruction of the Custom House and Assay Office. During the height of the fighting and under fire from both sides, the Assay Master and staff removed all the archives of the Company, the punches, and the office equipment to safety. On their last journey through the Custom House, they were arrested by the Crown forces and taken under escort to Dublin Castle.

The town mark of Dublin is Hibernia. The figure of Hibernia

was first used in 1730 to denote payment of special duty. In 1807, it was enacted that the Sovereign's Head should be stamped on gold and silver wrought in Ireland to show the payment of duty. This was discontinued on the repeal of the duty in 1890. The figure of Hibernia has, however, continued to be used since 1807 as a town mark. Between 1637 and 1807, the Harp mark served as a town mark and standard mark.

THE CLOSED OFFICES

CHESTER. The city of Chester figures in the history of craft from Saxon times. Documentary records of Chester goldsmiths are found from the 13th century.

The early history of the Chester guild is obscure, but some form of control and marking existed from early times and 17th-century pieces bearing Chester marks are known. From the beginning of the 18th century, regular assay and marking was carried out at the Chester Assay Office.

The early town mark of Chester was that in use to 1962, the arms of the City being Three Wheatsheaves and a Sword. Between 1701–2 and 1778–9, this crest was halved, with Three Lions, reverting on the latter date to the original, which is more distinctive and presents less difficulty to the punch cutter.

Additionally to the town mark, the Leopard's Head was in use from 1719–20 to 1838–9.

No great amount of wares of either gold or silver was manufactured in recent years in Chester and its neighbourhood, and the Office received daily consignments of gold and silver from manufacturers mainly in Birmingham.

The Office was eventually closed by statute in August 1962 and the last date letter, M, covers a period of a few weeks only.

GLASGOW. The Fish, Tree and Bell, with a Bird in the Branches of the Tree, form the town mark of Glasgow. The composition is difficult to include in a small punch, but the skill of the diesinker ensures that all these objects can be distinguished in even the smallest of Glasgow's later punches. In detail, the mark is composed of an oak tree with roots in the ground and spreading branches. Across the trunk of the tree is a salmon with a ring in its mouth, a hand-bell hangs from the lower tree branches, while on the topmost branch is perched a robin-redbreast. Again it is the city arms.

An Incorporation of Hammermen, which included the gold-

smiths with other workers in metals, was created in Glasgow in 1536. An Assay Office and the Glasgow Goldsmiths' Company were established by Act of Parliament in 1819, and the date letters of this city run from that year.

The Office was eventually closed in 1964.

OTHER CLOSED OFFICES

	Period of existence	Date letters used from	Town Mark	
EXETER	1701–1882/3	1544		
NEWCASTLE	1423–1863/4	1658		
YORK	1423–1856/7	1562/3		
NORWICH	1423–1697	1565/6		

THE MINOR GUILDS

There were small guilds of goldsmiths in England, Scotland and Ireland that had their own town marks. There is, however, no evidence that any Assay Office was ever established in these towns.

Some guilds started at a very early date, such as that in Barnstable which was marking plate from about 1370 to 1730, that in Lincoln from around 1420 to 1710, and that in Hull from about 1570 to 1710.

Others in Bristol, Kings Lynn, Leeds, Plymouth and Taunton, were operating from the first half of the 17th century to the beginning of the 18th.

In Scotland the minor guilds also flourished from an early time. There were about a dozen, that in Aberdeen having been active from as early as about 1450, and those in Perth and Dundee from about a century later. Most of the Scottish minor guilds finished marking in the first half of the 19th century, after the Glasgow Office was established.

In Ireland, small guilds in certain counties were active from about halfway through the 17th century until the 18th, or in two cases until the early 19th.

THE STERLING SILVER QUALITY MARK

Sterling silver is 92·5 per cent. pure silver, the rest being alloying metals. It is often shown as " 925/1000 ", which means 925 parts of fine silver in a total of a thousand parts. It is also indicated as " 11 ounces 2 pennyweights fine ", which means that weight of pure silver in a pound Troy of sterling silver.

Except for the purposes of hallmarking Statutes, pennyweights became no longer a legal measure after the beginning of 1969 under an enactment of the Weights and Measures Act of· 1963, and the pound Troy was dropped as a legal measure under an earlier enactment.

ENGLAND. The mark most expressive of the quality of sterling silver is undoubtedly the Lion Passant (passing by) which appears in the Hallmark for sterling silver of all the English Offices.

The exact origin of this mark is unknown. Its first appearance has been fixed at 1544, the period of the first debasement of the coinage from the sterling standard. It is conjectured that the mark was applied to announce the fact that, although the quality of silver in the coinage had declined, the goldsmiths maintained the sterling standard.

In his earliest portraits, the Lion Passant is guardant (with head turned) and wears a crown. The crown disappeared after a very short time. The guardant attitude was dropped from the London punch of 1821–2. The little lion, having by then lived among goldsmiths for nearly three hundred years, felt he could at least trust them and save the crick in his neck!

Birmingham turned the face forward in 1875–6, but on the marks of Chester until it was closed, and Sheffield until 1975, it still looked round.

SCOTLAND. Jackson* refers to a " Deacon's Mark " in use in Edinburgh after 1552 and an "Assay Master's Mark" from 1681–2 to 1758–9. The Assay Master was reponsible for guaranteeing the quality of the wares he marked by using an individual punch of his own as part of the hallmark.

From 1759–60 until recent times, a Thistle Flower with Two Leaves was used as the sterling quality mark for silver by the Edinburgh Assay Office, but at the beginning of 1975, a Lion Rampant, the lion of the Scottish Ensign, was introduced.

* " English Goldsmiths and their Marks," by Sir Charles Jackson.

The Lion Rampant was previously used by the Glasgow Assay Office from 1819. From 1914 the Thistle was added until the office was closed in 1964.

 REPUBLIC OF IRELAND. From 1637 to the present day, the Harp Crowned has been the fineness mark for sterling silver and 22 carat gold.

In addition, from 1637 to 1807, this mark had a dual purpose of being a town mark, too. From 1807 onwards the figure of Hibernia became the town mark for Dublin.

THE BRITANNIA SILVER QUALITY MARK

 To prevent the loss of coin in circulation owing to it being melted down to make into plate, William III, by Act of 1696, forbade the manufacture and hallmarking of plate of sterling quality (92·5 per cent.). The quality of the plate was raised to 95·8 per cent. fine.

 The new standard was distinguished by special marks: a Lion's Head Erased (heraldic lion's head in profile, jagged at the neck), and Britannia, the figure familiar on the 50p coin.

Britannia quality silver continued as the only silver for plate in use in England from 1697 to 1720, during part of the reign of William III, all of the reign of Queen Anne, and part of the reign of George I.

When the sterling standard was reintroduced, the Britannia standard was not dropped. It is still in occasional use and is assayed and marked by the Offices in Great Britain.

All the Assay Offices now use their normal town marks with the Britannia mark in place of the sterling silver mark, the Lion Passant —or Lion Rampant in the case of Edinburgh. Before the new regulations of 1975, however, London used the Lion's Head Erased as a town mark on this standard in place of the Leopard's Head; and Edinburgh and Glasgow in previous times used the regular sterling marks with the addition of the Britannia punch. The Britannia standard was never adopted in Ireland. The mark is therefore not found on Dublin marked plate.

THE DUTY MARK

 Articles of gold and silver hallmarked between 1784 and 1890— for 106 years—will normally be found to have five punch marks instead of four. The extra one is a duty mark showing the Sovereign's Head, that of George III, George IV, William IV, or Victoria. A full Hallmark of the period is shown below:

The duty was collected by the Assay Offices at the time of marking and the special punch mark denoted that it had been paid.

For a period of six months from July 15th, 1797, two heads were punched by the Sheffield Office to denote payment of double tax, and it may be that other Offices did the same.

OTHER ADDITIONAL MARKS

On two occasions, an additional punch has been added to the British Hallmark at the option of the owner of the articles offered for assay.

JUBILEE MARK. The first was to commemorate the 25th anniversary of the reign of King George V and Queen Mary and is known as the " Jubilee Mark ". It was first suggested by Arthur Tremayne who was the original compiler of this book.

The mark, showing the two crowned heads of the King and Queen side by side, was struck on silver only during the years 1933, 1934, and 1935.

CORONATION MARK. A similar punch, but showing the crowned head of Queen Elizabeth II facing to the right, was authorised for both silver and gold at the time of the coronation of the Queen.

Its use was also voluntary and it was struck only on wares which carried the date letter for 1952–3 or 1953–4.

SILVER JUBILEE MARK. An optional additional punch was used in 1977 on silver articles weighing 15 grams and over, to commemorate the silver jubilee of Queen Elizabeth II's accession. The date letter is C and a full mark for London is shown below.

1916–1966 IRISH JUBILEE MARK. To commemorate the golden jubilee of the 1916 rising, the Company of Goldsmiths of the Republic of Ireland authorised the striking of a commemorative mark on all items of gold and silver, other than jewellery and watch cases, marked in the year 1966.

 COMMEMORATIVE MARK. To denote the 350th anniversary of the Goldsmiths Company of Dublin, on all items of gold, silver and platinum marked in the year 1987 (letter B), except jewellery and watch cases.

HALLMARKS ON GOLD

The first mention of a legal standard for articles of gold is in the Act of Edward I, 1300, when gold was required to be of the quality of the " Touch of Paris ", equal to about 19 carat. It was composed of $19\frac{1}{5}$ parts pure gold and $4\frac{1}{5}$ parts alloy.

A full gold Hallmark will be similar to this.

Gold is alloyed with copper and silver to toughen and strengthen it. Equal quantities of copper and silver form a good alloy, but there are innumerable formulas used by manufacturers which include many other metals, each designed to produce alloyed gold of the required colour or other properties.

Gold can be yellow, red, or intermediate shades. It can be quite white, if palladium or nickel is used as the alloying metal, or even green. The full assayable quality of the gold must be maintained if the articles are to pass the Hall.

THE CARAT

" Carat " in hallmarking means the 24th part by weight of the whole. A gold dish of 18 carat weighing 48 ounces is 18/24 parts fine gold, *i.e.* there are 36 ounces of fine gold in it. An article of 22 carat gold has 22 parts fine gold in it and two parts of alloying metals.

The word " carat " used in the gem trade is quite different, as it is in this case a weight. A one carat diamond weighs one-fifth of a gram.

There is an ancient connection between the two. The Roman coin, the *solidus*, weighed 24 carats and was originally of pure gold, *i.e.* it was 24 carats of gold. When it was debased in *quality* it had less than 24 carats of gold in it, but still weighed 24 carats. This is how carat came to be used as a measure of quality.

LEGAL GOLD STANDARDS

Eighteen carat (three-quarters gold, one-quarter alloy) was the legal standard between 1477 and 1575. It was raised to 22 carat (22 parts gold, two parts alloy) in 1575 and this standard has never been altered.

Eighteen carat was again introduced as an additional standard in 1798, and in 1854 three more standards of 15 carat, 12 carat and 9 carat, were legalised.

The next—and so far, the last—change was in 1932 when the 15 carat and 12 carat standards were dropped and 14 carat substituted.

The gold standards now legal in Great Britain and Northern Ireland and the corresponding standard marks used on British made wares are:

	Before 1975	From Jan. 1, 1975
22 ct. (916·6 parts per 1000)	👑 22	👑 916
18 ct. (750 parts per 1000)	👑 18	👑 750
14 ct. (585 parts per 1000)	14 ·585	👑 585
9 ct. (375 parts per 1000)	9 375	👑 375

In Dublin the standards for gold are 22 ct. (91·66 per cent.), 20 ct. (83·3 per cent.)—first marked in Dublin in 1784, but rarely used, 18 ct. (75·0 per cent.), 14 ct. (58·5 per cent.), and 9 ct. (37·5 per cent.).

THE PLATINUM MARK

Platinum with a minimum fineness of 950 parts in 1000 was brought within Hallmarking law by the Act of 1973 from January 1, 1975. A new platinum mark showing an orb surmounted by a cross within a pentagon was introduced for articles made in the U.K. and the figures 950 for imported articles.

London and Birmingham began to assay platinum immediately and Sheffield from June 1975. A full platinum mark is shown above.

MARKS ON IMPORTED GOLD
AND SILVER

The quality of imported plate appears to have been uncontrolled until an Act of Victoria was passed in 1842, and revised in 1883. It provided that imported gold and silver wares should be assayed and hallmarked. A special punch " F " was added between 1876 and 1904 to indicate its foreign origin.

Since 1904 each Office has or had a special Assay Office mark for imported wares followed by a standard mark in figures and the usual date letter.

London   Birmingham   Sheffield   Chester   Edinburgh   Glasgow   Dublin

Assay Office marks on imported plate in use since May, 1906.

Standard marks on imported gold articles before August 15th, 1932.

*Standard marks on imported gold articles
from August 15th, 1932,
to January 1st, 1975.*

*Standard marks on imported silver articles
of Sterling and Britannia standards
before 1975.*

GOLD: **916** 22 carat   **750** 18 carat   **585** 14 carat   **375** 9 carat

SILVER: **958** Britannia   **925** Sterling   **950** PLATINUM

Standard marks on imported articles since 1975.

THE HALLMARKING COUNCIL

The Hallmarking Act of 1973 set up the British Hallmarking Council on January 1, 1974 to ensure adequate facilities for assay, to make sure the law on Hallmarking was enforced, and to advise the government.

THE INTERNATIONAL HALLMARK

On November 15, 1972, in Vienna, representatives of the governments of Austria, Finland, Norway, Portugal, Sweden, Switzerland, and the United Kingdom signed a convention on the Control and Marking of Articles of Precious Metals. It came into force in Austria, Finland, Sweden and Switzerland on June 27, 1975, and in the U.K. on April 1, 1976.

Articles bearing the Convention Hallmark may be sold in any of the signatory countries and described as gold, silver, or platinum as the case may be without the need for assay and Hallmarking by the country importing them.

Importing countries can still maintain their national standards, however. This means, for example, that continental 800 or 830 silver cannot legally be described as silver in the course of trade or business, despite its bearing the Convention Mark, because 925 (sterling) is the lowest UK standard.

| Sterling Silver | 18ct gold | 14ct gold | 9ct gold | Platinum | A full Convention Hallmark from Switzerland (Geneva) |

The Convention Hallmark comprises a sponsor's mark, a common control mark (one of those illustrated), a number indicating standard of fineness, and an Assay Office Mark.

THE ANTIQUE PLATE COMMITTEE

In 1939, the Worshipful Company of Goldsmiths, the responsible authority for the London Assay Office, set up a body of experts known as " The Antique Plate Committee " to advise on articles suspected of contravening the hallmarking law—for example, pieces bearing forged Hallmarks, or illegally altered articles.

This Committee meets regularly at Goldsmiths' Hall, Foster Lane, London E.C.2, and will examine free of charge any such articles submitted. Where possible, recommendations are made for bringing offending pieces within the law, such as the erasure of forged Hallmarks, after which the article can be assayed and, if up to standard, hallmarked as a new ware.

In fact, the number of spurious antique British silver wares in existence is quite small compared with the enormous quantity of perfectly genuine ones. This is due mainly to the protection afforded by the Hallmarking system.

EXAMPLES OF COMPLETE HALLMARKS

These are Pre-1975 marks as it is thought that most readers will be checking older silver. Post-1975 marks are included in the main text.

SILVER

LONDON

BRITISH SILVER WARES

	Makers' mark	Standard mark	Assay Office mark	Date letter
Sterling	AZ			b

	Makers' mark	Assay Office mark	Standard mark	Date letter
Britannia	AZ			b

FOREIGN SILVER WARES

	Assay Office mark	Standard mark	Date letter
Sterling		·925	b
Britannia		·9584	b

BIRMINGHAM

BRITISH SILVER WARES

	Makers' mark	Assay Office mark	Standard mark	Date letter
Sterling	AZ			H
Britannia	AZ			H

FOREIGN SILVER WARES

	Standard mark	Assay Office mark	Date letter
Sterling	·925	△	H
Britannia	·9584	△	H

SHEFFIELD

BRITISH SILVER WARES

	Makers' mark	Assay Office mark	Standard mark	Date letter
Sterling	AZ			P
Britannia	AZ			P

FOREIGN SILVER WARES

	Assay Office mark	Standard mark	Date letter
Sterling	♎	·925	P
Britannia	♎	·9584	P

EDINBURGH

BRITISH SILVER WARES

	Makers' mark	Standard mark	Assay Office mark	Date letter
Sterling	AZ			B
Britannia	AZ			B

FOREIGN SILVER WARES

	Standard mark	Assay Office mark	Date letter
Sterling	·925	X	B
Britannia	·9584	X	B

GOLD

LONDON

BRITISH GOLD WARES

	Makers' mark	Standard mark	Assay Office mark	Date letter
22 carat	AZ	22		b
18 carat	AZ	18		b

	Makers' mark	Assay Office mark	Date letter	Standard mark
14 carat	AZ	14 ·585	b	
9 carat	AZ	9 375	b	

FOREIGN GOLD WARES

	Date letter	Standard mark	Assay Office mark
22 carat	b	·916	
18 carat	b	750	
14 carat	b	·585	
9 carat	b	·375	

BIRMINGHAM

BRITISH GOLD WARES

	Makers' mark	Standard mark	Assay Office mark	Date letter
22 carat	AZ	22		H
18 carat	AZ	18		H
14 carat	AZ	14 ·585		H
9 carat	AZ	9 ·375		H

FOREIGN GOLD WARES

	Standard mark	Assay Office mark	Date letter
22 carat	·916	△	H
18 carat	750	△	H
14 carat	·585	△	H
9 carat	·375	△	H

SHEFFIELD

BRITISH GOLD WARES

	Makers' mark	Assay Office mark	Standard mark	Date letter
22 carat	AZ		22	P
18 carat	AZ		18	P
14 carat	AZ		14 ·585	P
9 carat	AZ		9 ·375	P

FOREIGN GOLD WARES

	Assay Office mark	Standard mark	Date letter
22 carat	Ω	·916	P
18 carat	Ω	750	P
14 carat	Ω	·585	P
9 carat	Ω	·375	P

EDINBURGH

BRITISH GOLD WARES

	Makers' mark	Standard mark	Assay Office mark	Date letter
22 carat	AZ	22		B
18 carat	AZ	18		B
14 carat	AZ	14 ·585		B
9 carat	AZ	9 ·375		B

FOREIGN GOLD WARES

	Standard mark	Assay Office mark	Date letter
22 carat	·916	X	B
18 carat	750	X	B
14 carat	·585	X	B
9 carat	·375	X	B

CLOSED OFFICES

CHESTER

BRITISH SILVER WARES

	Makers' mark	Standard mark	Assay Office mark	Date letter
Sterling				
Britannia				

FOREIGN SILVER WARES

	Assay Office mark	Standard mark	Date letter
Sterling			
Britannia			

GLASGOW

BRITISH SILVER WARES

	Makers' mark	Assay Office mark	Standard mark	Date letter	Standard mark
Sterling					
Britannia					

FOREIGN SILVER WARES

	Assay Office mark	Standard mark	Date letter
Sterling			
Britannia			

CHESTER

BRITISH GOLD WARES

	Makers' mark	Standard mark	Assay Office mark	Date letter
22 carat				
18 carat				

	Makers' mark	Assay Office mark	Standard mark	Date letter
14 carat				
9 carat				

FOREIGN GOLD WARES

	Assay Office mark	Standard mark	Date letter
22 carat			
18 carat			
14 carat			
9 carat			

GLASGOW

BRITISH GOLD WARES

	Makers' mark	Standard mark	Assay Office mark	Standard mark	Date letter
22 carat					
18 carat					
14 carat					
9 carat					

FOREIGN GOLD WARES

	Assay Office mark	Standard mark	Date letter
22 carat			
18 carat			
14 carat			
9 carat			

THE STANDARDS OF SILVER COIN

A.D.		Silver	Alloy
1300	Edward I	11 oz. 2 dwt.	18 dwt.
1542	Henry VIII	10 oz.	2 oz.
1544	,,	6 oz.	6 oz.
1545	,,	4 oz.	8 oz.
1549	Edward VI	6 oz.	6 oz.
1551	,,	3 oz.	9 oz.
1552	,,	11 oz. 1 dwt.	19 dwt.
1553	Mary	11 oz.	1 oz.
1560	Elizabeth	11 oz. 2 dwt.	18 dwt.
1920	George V	6 oz.	6 oz.
1947	George VI	Use of silver discontinued. Coins of cupro-nickel issued.	

LEGAL ENACTMENTS AND HISTORICAL FACTS
PLANTAGENET PERIOD

Reigning Sovereign	Date of Accession	Date of Act, etc.	
Henry II	Oct. 25 1154	1180	A Guild of Goldsmiths existed in London.
Richard I	July 6, 1189	—	
John	April 6, 1199	—	
Henry III	Oct. 19, 1216	1238	An ordinance regulated the standard of gold and silver wares.
,,	—	1300	A fixed standard prescribed for gold and silver. The minimum for gold being 19½ carat and, for silver, the sterling alloy.
Edward I	Nov. 16, 1272	1300	No silver wares to be sold until assayed and marked by the Guardians of the Craft, and the Guardians to assay gold wares.
Edward II	July 7, 1307	—	
Edward III	Jan. 25, 1327	1327	First charter granted to the Wardens and Commonalty of the Mystery of Goldsmiths of the City of London.
,,	—	1335	To preserve the supply of coinage within the realm, sterling must not be melted down or taken out of the country.
,,	—	1363	The maker's mark first mentioned. It was to be impressed on every article after the King's mark had been applied.

25

Reigning Sovereign	Date of Accession	Date of Act, etc.	
Richard II	June 22, 1377	1381	No gold or silver ware to be imported.
,,	—	1392–3	Second charter of London Goldsmiths.
Henry IV	Sept. 30, 1399	1403–4	The gilding and silvering of base metals, as copper and latten, is prohibited. Church vessels are exempt as long as some part of the base metal is left bare.
Henry V	March 21, 1413	1414	The gilding of silver permitted: but conditions of purity and price regulated.
Henry VI	Sept. 1, 1422	1423	York, Newcastle, Lincoln, Norwich, Bristol, Salisbury and Coventry were given individual " touches ". Chester is not mentioned probably because its touch was already well established.
,,	—	1423	Heavy penalties prescribed if the Keeper of the Touch passes silver of a lower standard than sterling.
,,	—	1423	The price of silver fixed at 22s per pound.
Edward IV	March 4, 1461	1462	Third charter of London Goldsmiths.
,,	—	1477	The standard of gold reduced from 19⅕ to 18 carat.
,,	—	1478	First mention of the Leopard's Head being crowned.
,,	—	1478	No gold ware to be of less than 18 carat and no silver less than sterling.
,;	—	1479	A silver article is in existence, known to belong to this year, bearing the date letter B.
Edward V	April 9, 1483	—	
Richard III	June 26, 1483	—	

TUDOR PERIOD

Henry VII	Aug. 22, 1485	1500	A guild or mystery of goldsmiths known to exist in Exeter about this time, but it had no statutory authority.
Henry VIII	April 22, 1509	1526–7	The old Tower pound by which silver had been weighed is abolished.
,,	—	1536	A charter granted to the goldsmiths of Newcastle.
,,	—	1544	First known appearance of the Lion Passant as a sterling quality mark in England.

Reigning Sovereign	Date of Accession	Date of Act, etc.	
Edward VI	Jan. 28, 1547	—	
Mary	July 6, 1553		
Elizabeth	Nov. 17, 1558	1572	The Exeter town mark—a Roman letter X or an X crowned with a mullet on either side.
,,	—	1576	The standard of gold raised from 18 to 22 carat.
,,	—	1576	An Act imposing penalties on makers if their mark is not stamped on their work. No specific mention made as to the need for official marks.

STUART AND PURITAN PERIODS

James I	March 24, 1603	1610	The Norwich touch changed from a castle and lion to a crowned double-seeded rose.
Charles I	March 27, 1625	1625–49	Very little plate made during this reign owing to the Civil War.
,,	—	1632	York. The mark changed from a " halfe leopard head and half floure-de-luce " to a " half rose crowned and half fleur-de-lis ".
Common-wealth	Cromwell made Protector Dec. 16, 1653		
Charles II	May 26, 1660		
James II	Feb. 6, 1685		

WILLIAM AND MARY PERIOD

William and Mary	Feb. 13, 1689 Mary died Dec. 28, 1694	1689	The Civil War being ended, silver articles became in great demand, even for tankards in taverns. Consequently, silver coin became scarce. This led to the passing of an Act requiring all extracted gold and silver to be used for increasing the currency.
,,	—	1694–5	No bullion to be exported unless proof could be given that it had never been in the form of coin.
William III	—	1695–6	No tavern or inn to make use of silver tankards, etc. Silver spoons were, however, permitted.
,,	—	1697	The standard of silver ware raised from 11 oz. 2 dwt. to 11 oz. 10 dwt. in the lb. troy and the Britannia mark substituted for the Leopard's Head (on silver only).

27

Reigning Sovereign	Date of Accession	Date of Act, etc.	
William III	—	1697	Very small articles need not be stamped, if the stamp is likely to deface them.
,,	—	1697	The maker's mark which, hitherto, had often been an outline drawing was now to consist of the first two letters of the maker's surname.
,,	—	1697	Norwich Assay office closed.
,,	—	1701	Statutory powers first accorded to Bristol, Chester, Exeter, Norwich and York. Norwich, however, did not avail itself of the privilege.

QUEEN ANNE PERIOD

Anne	March 8, 1702	1702	Similar privileges given to Newcastle.

GEORGIAN PERIOD

George I	Aug. 1, 1714	1719	Much silver having been captured from the Spaniards and good supplies coming from the East Indies, the Britannia standard became no longer compulsory. Henceforth, the Leopard's Head and the Britannia mark could both be used for their respective standards.
,,	—	1719	For the Britannia standard of silver, the maker's mark to consist of the first two letters of the maker's surname. For the lower standard, the mark to consist of his initials.
,,	—	1719	A duty of 6d. oz. imposed on all silver wares wrought in G.B.
George II	June 11, 1727	1738	Penalties increased for making articles of lower than statutory standard, as cases of fraud were on the increase.
,,	—	1739	The maker's mark to consist of the maker's initials. Relevant section of Act of 1719 cancelled.
,,	—	1757–8	The duty of 6d. oz. on silver wares repealed. Instead, a licence tax of 40s. per annum substituted.

Cont.

LONDON DATE LETTERS

Year – No.	Year – No.	Year – No.	Year – No.	Year – No.	Year – No.
1660 – 1	1693 – 4	1726 – 7	1758 – 9	1791 – 2	1824 – 5
1661 – 2	1694 – 5	1727 – 8	1759 – 0	1792 – 3	1825 – 6
1662 – 3	1695 – 6	1728 – 9	1760 – 1	1793 – 4	1826 – 7
1663 – 4	1696 – 7	1729 – 0	1761 – 2	1794 – 5	1827 – 8
1664 – 5	1697 – 8	1730 – 1	1762 – 3	1795 – 6	1828 – 9
1665 – 6	1698 – 9	1731 – 2	1763 – 4	1796 – 7	1829 – 0
1666 – 7	1699 – 0	1732 – 3	1764 – 5	1797 – 8	1830 – 1
1667 – 8	1700 – 1	1733 – 4	1765 – 6	1798 – 9	1831 – 2
1668 – 9	1701 – 2	1734 – 5	1766 – 7	1799 – 0	1832 – 3
1669 – 0	1702 – 3	1735 – 6	1767 – 8	1800 – 1	1833 – 4
1670 – 1	1703 – 4	1736 – 7	1768 – 9	1801 – 2	1834 – 5
1671 – 2	1704 – 5	1737 – 8	1769 – 0	1802 – 3	1835 – 6
1672 – 3	1705 – 6	1738 – 9	1770 – 1	1803 – 4	1836 – 7
1673 – 4	1706 – 7	1739 – 0	1771 – 2	1804 – 5	1837 – 8
1674 – 5	1707 – 8	1739 – 0	1772 – 3	1805 – 6	1838 – 9
1675 – 6	1708 – 9	1740 – 1	1773 – 4	1806 – 7	1839 – 0
1676 – 7	1709 – 0	1741 – 2	1774 – 5	1807 – 8	1840 – 1
1677 – 8	1710 – 1	1742 – 3	1775 – 6	1808 – 9	1841 – 2
1678 – 9	1711 – 2	1743 – 4	1776 – 7	1809 – 0	1842 – 3
1679 – 0	1712 – 3	1744 – 5	1777 – 8	1810 – 1	1843 – 4
1680 – 1	1713 – 4	1745 – 6	1778 – 9	1811 – 2	1844 – 5
1681 – 2	1714 – 5	1746 – 7	1779 – 0	1812 – 3	1845 – 6
1682 – 3	1715 – 6	1747 – 8	1780 – 1	1813 – 4	1846 – 7
1683 – 4	1716 – 7	1748 – 9	1781 – 2	1814 – 5	1847 – 8
1684 – 5	1717 – 8	1749 – 0	1782 – 3	1815 – 6	1848 – 9
1685 – 6	1718 – 9	1750 – 1	1783 – 4	1816 – 7	1849 – 0
1686 – 7	1719 – 0	1751 – 2	1784 – 5	1817 – 8	1850 – 1
1687 – 8	1720 – 1	1752 – 3	1785 – 6	1818 – 9	1851 – 2
1688 – 9	1721 – 2	1753 – 4	1786 – 7	1819 – 0	1852 – 3
1689 – 0	1722 – 3	1754 – 5	1787 – 8	1820 – 1	1853 – 4
1690 – 1	1723 – 4	1755 – 6	1788 – 9	1821 – 2	1854 – 5
1691 – 2	1724 – 5	1756 – 7	1789 – 0	1822 – 3	1855 – 6
1692 – 3	1725 – 6	1757 – 8	1790 – 1	1823 – 4	1856 – 7

29

b 1857 – 8	O 1889 – 0	f 1921 – 2	S 1953 – 4	H 1982
c 1858 – 9	P 1890 – 1	g 1922 – 3	T 1954 – 5	J 1983
d 1859 – 0	Q 1891 – 2	h 1923 – 4	U 1955 – 6	K 1984
e 1860 – 1	R 1892 – 3	i 1924 – 5	a 1956 – 7	L 1985
f 1861 – 2	S 1893 – 4	k 1925 – 6	b 1957 – 8	M 1986
g 1862 – 3	T 1894 – 5	l 1926 – 7	c 1958 – 9	N 1987
h 1863 – 4	U 1895 – 6	m 1927 – 8	d 1959 – 60	O 1988
i 1864 – 5	a 1896 – 7	n 1928 – 9	e 1960 – 1	
k 1865 – 6	b 1897 – 8	o 1929 – 0	f 1961 – 2	
l 1866 – 7	c 1898 – 9	p 1930 – 1	g 1962 – 3	
m 1867 – 8	d 1899 – 0	q 1931 – 2	h 1963 – 4	
n 1868 – 9	e 1900 – 1	r 1932 – 3	i 1964 – 5	
o 1869 – 0	f 1901 – 2	s 1933 – 4	k 1965 – 6	
p 1870 – 1	g 1902 – 3	t 1934 – 5	l 1966 – 7	
q 1871 – 2	h 1903 – 4	u 1935 – 6	m 1967 – 8	
r 1872 – 3	i 1904 – 5	A 1936 – 7	n 1968 – 9	
s 1873 – 4	k 1905 – 6	B 1937 – 8	O 1969 – 70	
t 1874 – 5	l 1906 – 7	C 1938 – 9	P 1970 – 1	
u 1875 – 6	m 1907 – 8	D 1939 – 0	Q 1971 – 2	
A 1876 – 7	n 1908 – 9	E 1940 – 1	r 1972 – 3	
B 1877 – 8	o 1909 – 0	F 1941 – 2	S 1973 – 4	
C 1878 – 9	p 1910 – 1	G 1942 – 3	t 1974	
D 1879 – 0	q 1911 – 2	H 1943 – 4	From Jan 1st 1975 as all UK Offices	
E 1880 – 1	r 1912 – 3	I 1944 – 5	A 1975	
F 1881 – 2	s 1913 – 4	K 1945 – 6	B 1976	
G 1882 – 3	t 1914 – 5	L 1946 – 7	C 1977	
H 1883 – 4	u 1915 – 6	M 1947 – 8	D 1978	
I 1884 – 5	a 1916 – 7	N 1948 – 9	E 1979	
K 1885 – 6	b 1917 – 8	O 1949 – 50	F 1980	
L 1886 – 7	c 1918 – 9	P 1950 – 1	G 1981	
M 1887 – 8	d 1919 – 0	Q 1951 – 2		
N 1888 – 9	e 1920 – 1	R 1952 – 3		

Birmingham Date Letters Cont

W 1971 – 2
X 1972 – 3
Y 1973 – 4
Z July – Dec 1974

From Jan 1st 1975 as all UK Offices See London

A 1773 – 4	i 1806 – 7	Q 1839 – 0	X 1872 – 3	f 1905 – 6	O 1938 – 9
B 1774 – 5	j 1807 – 8	R 1840 – 1	Y 1873 – 4	g 1906 – 7	P 1939 – 0
C 1775 – 6	k 1808 – 9	S 1841 – 2	Z 1874 – 5	h 1907 – 8	Q 1940 – 1
D 1776 – 7	l 1809 – 0	T 1842 – 3	a 1875 – 6	i 1908 – 9	R 1941 – 2
E 1777 – 8	m 1810 – 1	U 1843 – 4	b 1876 – 7	k 1909 – 0	S 1942 – 3
F 1778 – 9	n 1811 – 2	W 1844 – 5	c 1877 – 8	l 1910 – 1	T 1943 – 4
G 1779 – 0	o 1812 – 3	W 1845 – 6	d 1878 – 9	m 1911 – 2	U 1944 – 5
H 1780 – 1	p 1813 – 4	X 1846 – 7	e 1879 – 0	n 1912 – 3	V 1945 – 6
I 1781 – 2	q 1814 – 5	Y 1847 – 8	f 1880 – 1	o 1913 – 4	W 1946 – 7
K 1782 – 3	r 1815 – 6	Z 1848 – 9	g 1881 – 2	p 1914 – 5	X 1947 – 8
L 1783 – 4	s 1816 – 7	A 1849 – 0	h 1882 – 3	q 1915 – 6	Y 1948 – 9
M 1784 – 5	t 1817 – 8	B 1850 – 1	i 1883 – 4	r 1916 – 7	Z 1949 – 50
N 1785 – 6	u 1818 – 9	C 1851 – 2	k 1884 – 5	s 1917 – 8	A 1950 – 1
O 1786 – 7	v 1819 – 0	D 1852 – 3	l 1885 – 6	t 1918 – 9	B 1951 – 2
P 1787 – 8	w 1820 – 1	E 1853 – 4	m 1886 – 7	u 1919 – 0	C 1952 – 3
Q 1788 – 9	x 1821 – 2	F 1854 – 5	n 1887 – 8	v 1920 – 1	D 1953 – 4
R 1789 – 0	y 1822 – 3	G 1855 – 6	o 1888 – 9	w 1921 – 2	E 1954 – 5
S 1790 – 1	z 1823 – 4	H 1856 – 7	p 1889 – 0	x 1922 – 3	F 1955 – 6
T 1791 – 2	a 1824 – 5	I 1857 – 8	q 1890 – 1	y 1923 – 4	G 1956 – 7
U 1792 – 3	b 1825 – 6	J 1858 – 9	r 1891 – 2	z 1924 – 5	H 1957 – 8
V 1793 – 4	c 1826 – 7	K 1859 – 0	s 1892 – 3	A 1925 – 6	J 1958 – 9
W 1794 – 5	d 1827 – 8	L 1860 – 1	t 1893 – 4	B 1926 – 7	K 1959 – 60
X 1795 – 6	e 1828 – 9	M 1861 – 2	u 1894 – 5	C 1927 – 8	L 1960 – 1
Y 1796 – 7	f 1829 – 0	N 1862 – 3	v 1895 – 6	D 1928 – 9	M 1961 – 2
Z 1797 – 8	g 1830 – 1	O 1863 – 4	w 1896 – 7	E 1929 – 0	N 1962 – 3
a 1798 – 9	h 1831 – 2	P 1864 – 5	x 1897 – 8	F 1930 – 1	O 1963 – 4
b 1799 – 0	j 1832 – 3	Q 1865 – 6	y 1898 – 9	G 1931 – 2	P 1964 – 5
c 1800 – 1	k 1833 – 4	R 1866 – 7	z 1899 – 0	H 1932 – 3	Q 1965 – 6
d 1801 – 2	l 1834 – 5	S 1867 – 8	a 1900 – 1	J 1933 – 4	R 1966 – 7
e 1802 – 3	m 1835 – 6	T 1868 – 9	b 1901 – 2	K 1934 – 5	S 1967 – 8
f 1803 – 4	n 1836 – 7	U 1869 – 0	c 1902 – 3	L 1935 – 6	T 1968 – 9
g 1804 – 5	o 1837 – 8	V 1870 – 1	d 1903 – 4	M 1936 – 7	U 1969 – 70
h 1805 – 6	p 1838 – 9	W 1871 – 2	e 1904 – 5	N 1937 – 8	V 1970 – 1

Cont. opposite

Letter	Year	Letter	Year	Letter	Year	Letter	Year	Letter	Year	Letter	Year
C	1773–4	X	1797–8	g	1830–1	V	1863–4	d	1896–7	m	1929–0
F	1774–5	V	1798–9	h	1831–2	W	1864–5	e	1897–8	n	1930–1
Ω	1775–6	E	1799–0	k	1832–3	X	1865–6	f	1898–9	o	1931–2
R	1776–7	N	1800–1	l	1833–4	Y	1866–7	g	1899–0	p	1932–3
D	1777–8	H	1801–2	m	1834–5	Z	1867–8	h	1900–1	q	1933–4
S	1778–9	M	1802–3	p	1835–6	A	1868–9	i	1901–2	r	1934–5
A	1779–0	F	1803–4	q	1836–7	B	1869–0	k	1902–3	s	1935–6
C	1780–1	G	1804–5	r	1837–8	C	1870–1	l	1903–4	t	1936–7
		B	1805–	s	1838–9	D	1871–2	m	1904–5	u	1937–8
		A	1806–7	t	1839–0	E	1872–3	n	1905–6	v	1938–9
		S	1807–8	u	1840–1	F	1873–4	o	1906–7	w	1939–0
		P	1808–9	v	1841–2	G	1874–5	p	1907–8	x	1940–1
		K	1809–0	x	1842–3	H	1875–6	q	1908–9	y	1941–2
		L	1810–1	z	1843–4	J	1876–7	r	1909–0	z	1942–3
		C	1811–2	A	1844–5	K	1877–8	s	1910–1	A	1943–4
		D	1812–3	B	1845–6	L	1878–9	t	1911–2	B	1944–5
		R	1813–4	C	1846–7	M	1879–0	u	1912–3	C	1945–6
D	1781–2	W	1814–5	D	1847–8	N	1880–1	v	1913–4	D	1946–7
G	1782–3	O	1815–6	E	1848–9	O	1881–2	w	1914–5	E	1947–8
B	1783–4	T	1816–7	F	1849–0	P	1882–3	x	1915–6	F	1948–9
J	1784–5	X	1817–8	G	1850–1	Q	1883–4	y	1916–7	G	1949–50
P	1785–6	I	1818–9	H	1851–2	R	1884–5	3	1917–8	H	1950–1
R	1786–7	V	1819–0	I	1852–3	S	1885–6	a	1918–9	I	1951–2
T	1787–8	Q	1820–1	K	1853–4	T	1886–7	b	1919–0	K	1952–3
W	1788–9	Y	1821–2	L	1854–5	U	1887–8	c	1920–1	L	1953–4
M	1789–0	Z	1822–3	M	1855–6	V	1888–9	d	1921–2	M	1954–5
I	1790–1	U	1823–4	N	1856–7	W	1889–0	e	1922–3	N	1955–6
P	1791–2	a	1824–5	O	1857–8	X	1890–1	f	1923–4	O	1956–7
U	1792–3	b	1825–6	P	1858–9	Y	1891–2	g	1924–5	P	1957–8
O	1793–4	c	1826–7	R	1859–0	Z	1892–3	h	1925–6	Q	1958–9
m	1794–5	d	1827–8	S	1860–1	a	1893–4	i	1926–7	R	1959–60
q	1795–6	e	1828–9	T	1861–2	b	1894–5	k	1927–8	S	1960–61
Z	1796–7	f	1829–0	U	1862–3	c	1895–6	l	1928–9		

Between 1780–1 and 1853–4 the Crown and Date Letter was included in one punch in the smaller sizes until 1828–9 as [Q] or [C] and after [of] or [Eo] or [op]

SHEFFIELD DATE LETTERS

1961 – 2	W 1964 – 5	Z 1967 – 8	C 1970 – 1	Œ 1973 – 4	From Jan. 1st. 1975
U 1962 – 3	X 1965 – 6	𝒜 1968 – 9	D 1971 – 2	G 1974 – 5	as all UK Offices
V 1963 – 4	Y 1966 – 7	B 1969 – 70	ℰ 1972 – 3		See London

GEORGIAN PERIOD—*continued*

Reigning Sovereign	Date of Accession	Date of Act, etc.	
George II	—	1757–8	The counterfeiting of dies and marks punishable by death.
,,	—	1759	The licence raised to £5 but small craftsmen are exempted.
,,	—	1759	First use noted of the Thistle as the sterling quality mark for Scotland.
George III	Oct. 25, 1760	1773	Birmingham and Sheffield become Assay offices by statute. The Sheffield town mark is a crown, Birmingham an anchor.
,,	—	1773	The death penalty (*See 1757-8*) reduced to transportation for 14 years.
,,	—	1784	The duty of 6d. per oz. on silver re-imposed. Also a duty of 8s. per oz. is imposed on gold. The Sovereign's head or " duty mark " to be impressed on all but certain gold and silver articles.
,,	—	1796	The duty on silver raised from 6d. to 1s. per oz.
,,	—	1797	Watch cases exempted from duty.
,,	—	1797	Additional standard of 18 carat introduced for gold. Marks to be crown and figure 18. Lion Passant not used for this standard.
,,	—	1798	No gold assayed at York after this date.
,,	—	1803	The duty on gold increased to 16s. per oz. and on silver wares to 1s. 3d.
,,	—	1814–15	Duty on gold increased to 17s. per oz. and on silver wares to 1s. 6d.
George IV	Jan. 29, 1820	1821	The Leopard's Head appears uncrowned and without a flowing mane.
William IV	June 26, 1830	—	*Cont.*

33

CHESTER DATE LETTERS

Letter	Year	Letter	Year	Letter	Year	Letter	Year	Letter	Year	Letter	Year
A	1701–2	J	1734–5	R	1767–8	D	1800–1	P	1833–4	t	1866–7
B	1702–3	K	1735–6	S	1768–9	E	1801–2	Q	1834–5	d	1867–8
C	1703–4	L	1736–7	T	1769–0	F	1802–3	R	1835–6	e	1868–9
D	1704–5	M	1737–8	TT	1770–1	G	1803–4	S	1836–7	f	1869–0
E	1705–6	N	1738–9	U	1771–2	H	1804–5	T	1837–8	g	1870–1
F	1706–7	O	1739–0	V	1772–3	I	1805–6	U	1838–9	h	1871–2
G	1707–8	P	1740–1	W	1773–4	K	1806–7	a	1839–0	i	1872–3
H	1708–9	Q	1741–2	X	1774–5	L	1807–8	B	1840–1	k	1873–4
I	1709–0	R	1742–3	Y	1775–6	M	1808–9	C	1841–2	l	1874–5
K	1710–1	S	1743–4	a	1776–7	N	1809–0	D	1842–3	m	1875–6
L	1711–2	T	1744–5	b	1777–8	O	1810–1	E	1843–4	n	1876–7
M	1712–3	U	1745–6	c	1778–9	P	1811–2	F	1844–5	o	1877–8
N	1713–4	V	1746–7	d	1779–0	Q	1812–3	G	1845–6	p	1878–9
O	1714–5	W	1747–8	e	1780–1	R	1813–4	H	1846–7	q	1879–0
P	1715–6	X	1748–9	f	1781–2	S	1814–5	I	1847–8	r	1880–1
Q	1716–7	Y/Y	1749–0	g	1782–3	T	1815–6	K	1848–9	s	1881–2
R	1717–8	Z	1750–1	h	1783–4	U	1816–7	L	1849–0	t	1882–3
S	1718–9	a	1751–2	i	1784–5	V	1817–8	M	1850–1	u	1883–4
T	1719–0	b	1752–3	k	1785–6	A	1818–9	N	1851–2	A	1884–5
U	1720–1	c	1753–4	l	1786–7	B	1819–0	O	1852–3	B	1885–6
V	1721–2	d	1754–5	m	1787–8	C	1820–1	P	1853–4	C	1886–7
W	1722–3	e	1755–6	n	1788–9	D	1821–2	Q	1854–5	D	1887–8
X	1723–4	f	1756–7	o	1789–0	D	1822–3	R	1855–6	E	1888–9
Y	1724–5	g	1757–8	p	1790–1	E	1823–4	S	1856–7	F	1889–0
Z	1725–6	h	1758–9	q	1791–2	F	1824–5	T	1857–8	G	1890–1
A	1726–7	i	1759–0	r	1792–3	G	1825–6	U	1858–9	H	1891–2
B	1727–8	k	1760–1	s	1793–4	H	1826–7	V	1859–0	I	1892–3
C	1728–9	l	1761–2	t	1794–5	I	1827–8	W	1860–1	K	1893–4
D	1729–0	m	1762–3	u	1795–6	K	1828–9	X	1861–2	L	1894–5
E	1730–1	n	1763–4	v	1796–7	L	1829–0	Y	1862–3	M	1895–6
F	1731–2	O	1764–5	A	1797–8	M	1830–1	Z	1863–4	N	1896–7
G	1732–3	P	1765–6	B	1798–9	N	1831–2	a	1864–5	O	1897–8
H	1733–4	Q	1766–7	C	1799–0	O	1832–3	b	1865–6	P	1898–9

CHESTER DATE LETTERS

Letter	Date	Letter	Date	Letter	Date	Letter	Date	Letter	Date	Letter	Date
Q	1899 – 0	H	1908 – 9	U	1920 – 1	g	1932 – 3	S	1943 – 4	D	1954 – 5
R	1900 – 1	J	1909 – 0	V	1921 – 2	h	1933 – 4	T	1944 – 5	E	1955 – 6
A	1901 – 2	K	1910 – 1	W	1922 – 3	J	1934 – 5	U	1945 – 6	F	1956 – 7
After 1901 Large Shields ◯		X	1923 – 4	R	1935 – 6	V	1946 – 7	G	1957 – 8
Small Shields ◯		L	1911 – 2	Y	1924 – 5	k	1936 – 7	W	1947 – 8	H	1958 – 9
		M	1912 – 3	Z	1925 – 6	m	1937 – 8	X	1948 – 9	J	1959 – 60
B	1902 – 3	N	1913 – 4	a	1926 – 7	n	1938 – 9	Y	1949 – 50	K	1960 – 1
C	1903 – 4	O	1914 – 5	b	1927 – 8	o	1939 – 0	Z	1950 – 1	L	1961 – 2
D	1904 – 5	P	1915 – 6	c	1928 – 9	p	1940 – 1	A	1951 – 2	M	1962 – 3
E	1905 – 6	Q	1916 – 7	d	1929 – 0	q	1941 – 2	B	1952 – 3	Closed 1962
F	1906 – 7	R	1917 – 8	e	1930 – 1	r	1942 – 3	C	1953 – 4	
G	1907 – 8	J	1918 – 9	ff	1931 – 2						
		T	1919 – 0								

VICTORIAN PERIOD AND AFTER

Reigning Sovereign	Date of Accession	Date of Act, etc.	
Victoria	June 20, 1837	1842	No imported gold or silver ware to be sold until it has been assayed and marked in this country.
,,	—	1844	Affixing to any ware a fraudulent mark or one cut from another piece is, by a new Act, a felony.
,,	—	1854	To be able to compete in foreign markets, three new standards for gold are established, i.e., 15, 12 and 9 carat.
,,	—	1856–7	York Assay office closed.
,,	—	1883	All foreign wares imported for sale to be assayed in this country and marked as though made here, but to bear an additional **F** mark.
,,	—	1883	Exeter Assay office closed.
,,	—	1884	Newcastle Assay office closed.
,,	—	1890	Duty on gold and silver wares abolished and the duty mark disappears.
Edward VII	Jan. 22, 1901	1904–6	The **F** foreign mark (See *1883*) was replaced by distinctive marks for each Assay office.

Cont.

35

Letter	Year	Letter	Year	Letter	Year	Letter	Year	Letter	Year	Letter	Year
a	1681–2	K	1714–5	S	1747–8	A	1780–1	h	1813–4	P	1846–7
b	1682–3	L	1715–6	T	1748–9	B	1781–2	i	1814–5	Q	1847–8
c	1683–4	M	1716–7	U	1749–0	C	1782–3	j	1815–6	R	1848–9
d	1684–5	N	1717–8	V	1750–1	D	1783–4	k	1816–7	S	1849–0
e	1685–6	O	1718–9	W	1751–2	E	1784–5	l	1817–8	T	1850–1
f	1686–7	P P	1719–0	X	1752–3	F	1785–6	m	1818–9	U	1851–2
g	1687–8	Q	1720–1	Y	1753–4	G	1786–7	n	1819–0	V	1852–3
h	1688–9	R	1721–2	Z	1754–5	G	1787–8	o	1820–1	W	1853–4
i	1689–0	S	1722–3	A	1755–6	H	1788–9	p	1821–2	X	1854–5
k	1690–1	T	1723–4	B	1756–7	I J	1789–0	q	1822–3	Y	1855–6
l	1691–2	U	1724–5	C	1757–8	K	1790–1	r	1823–4	Z	1856–7
m	1692–3	V V	1725–6	D	1758–9	L	1791–2	s	1824–5	A	1857–8
n	1693–4	W	1726–7	E	1759–0	M	1792–3	t	1825–6	B	1858–9
o	1694–5	X	1727–8	F	1760–1	N N	1793–4	u	1826–7	C	1859–0
p	1695–6	Y	1728–9	G	1761–2	O O	1794–5	v	1827–8	D	1860–1
q	1696–7	Z	1729–0	H	1762–3	P	1795–6	w	1828–9	E	1861–2
r	1697–8	A	1730–1	I I	1763–4	Q	1796–7	x	1829–0	F	1862–3
s	1698–9	B	1731–2	K	1764–5	R R	1797–8	y	1830–1	G	1863–4
t	1699–0	C	1732–3	L	1765–6	S	1798–9	z	1831–2	H	1864–5
u	1700–1	D	1733–4	M	1766–7	T	1799–0	a	1832–3	I	1865–6
w	1701–2	E	1734–5	N	1767–8	U	1800–1	b	1833–4	K	1866–7
x	1702–3	F	1735–6	O	1768–9	V	1801–2	c	1834–5	L	1867–8
y	1703–4	G	1736–7	P	1769–0	W	1802–3	d	1835–6	M	1868–9
z	1704–5	H	1737–8	Q	1770–1	X	1803–4	e	1836–7	N	1869–0
A	1705–6	I	1738–9	R	1771–2	Y	1804–5	f	1837–8	O	1870–1
B	1706–7	K	1739–0	S	1772–3	Z	1805–6	g	1838–9	P	1871–2
C	1707–8	L	1740–1	T	1773–4	a	1806–7	h	1839–0	Q	1872–3
D	1708–9	M	1741–2	U	1774–5	b	1807–8	j	1840–1	R	1873–4
E	1709–0	N	1742–3	V	1775–6	c	1808–9	k	1841–2	S	1874–5
F	1710–1	O	1743–4	X	1776–7	d	1809–0	l	1842–3	T	1875–6
G	1711–2	P	1744–5	P	1777–8	e	1810–1	M	1843–4	U	1876–7
H	1712–3	Q	1745–6	Z	1778–9	f	1811–2	N	1844–5	V	1877–8
I	1713–4	R	1746–7	V	1779–0	g	1812–3	O	1845–6	W	1878–9

EDINBURGH DATE LETTERS

Letter	Year	Letter	Year	Letter	Year	Letter	Year	Letter	Year	Letter	Year
Ⓧ	1879 – 0	Ⓞ	1895 – 6	Ⓕ	1911 – 2	Ⓦ	1927 – 8	𝒩	1943 – 4	Ⓓ	1959–60
Ⓨ	1880 – 1	Ⓟ	1896 – 7	Ⓖ	1912 – 3	Ⓧ	1928 – 9	𝒪	1944 – 5	Ⓔ	1960–1
Ⓩ	1881 – 2	Ⓠ	1897 – 8	Ⓗ	1913 – 4	Ⓨ	1929 – 0	𝒫	1945 – 6	Ⓕ	1961–2
ⓐ	1882 – 3	Ⓡ	1898 – 9	Ⓘ	1914 – 5	Ⓩ	1930 – 1	𝒬	1946 – 7	Ⓖ	1962–3
ⓑ	1883 – 4	Ⓢ	1899 – 0	Ⓚ	1915 – 6	𝒜	1931 – 2	ℛ	1947 – 8	Ⓝ	1963–4
ⓒ	1884 – 5	Ⓣ	1900 – 1	Ⓛ	1916 – 7	ℬ	1932 – 3	𝒮	1948 – 9	Λ	1964–5
ⓓ	1885 – 6	Ⓤ	1901 – 2	Ⓜ	1917 – 8	𝒞	1933 – 4	𝒯	1949 – 0	Ⓚ	1965–6
ⓔ	1886 – 7	Ⓦ	1902 – 3	Ⓝ	1918 – 9	𝒟	1934 – 5	𝒰	1950 – 1	Ⓛ	1966–7
ⓕ	1887 – 8	Ⓧ	1903 – 4	Ⓞ	1919 – 0	ℰ	1935 – 6	𝒱	1951–2	Ⓜ	1967–8
ⓖ	1888 – 9	Ⓟ	1904 – 5	Ⓟ	1920 – 1	ℱ	1936 – 7	𝒲	1952–3	Ⓝ	1968–9
ⓗ	1889 – 0	Ⓩ	1905 – 6	Ⓠ	1921 – 2	𝒢	1937 – 8	𝒳	1953–4	Ⓞ	1969 – 70
ⓘ	1890 – 1	Ⓐ	1906 – 7	Ⓡ	1922 – 3	ℋ	1938 – 9	𝒴	1954–5	Ⓟ	1970 – 1
ⓚ	1891 – 2	Ⓑ	1907 – 8	Ⓢ	1923 – 4	𝒥	1939 – 0	𝒵	1955–6	Ⓠ	1971 – 2
ⓛ	1892 – 3	Ⓒ	1908 – 9	Ⓣ	1924 – 5	𝒦	1940 – 1	Ⓐ	1956–7	Ⓡ	1972 – 3
ⓜ	1893 – 4	Ⓓ	1909 – 0	Ⓤ	1925 – 6	ℒ	1941 – 2	Ⓑ	1957–8	Ⓢ	1973 – 4
ⓝ	1894 – 5	Ⓔ	1910 – 1	Ⓥ	1926 – 7	ℳ	1942 – 3	Ⓒ	1958–9	Then as London

Reigning Sovereign	Date of Accession	Date of Act, etc.	
George V	May 6, 1910	1932	A new standard of 14 ct. introduced for gold and the use of the old standards of 12 ct. and 15 ct. abolished.
,,	—	1935	Silver Jubilee Mark. An additional mark applied voluntarily to silver during period Feb. 6–Dec. 31, 1935.
Edward VIII	Jan. 20, 1936	—	
George VI	Dec. 11, 1936	—	
,,	—	1939	Hallmarking of Foreign Plate Act. Allowed foreign wares proved to be more than 100 years old to be sold unhallmarked.
George VI	—	1951	Common Informers Act. Abolished the common inform procedure in hallmarking prosecutions.
Elizabeth II	Feb. 6, 1952	1953	Coronation Mark. An additional mark applied voluntarily with date letters for 1952–3 and 1953–4.
,,	—	1962	Chester Assay office closed.
,,	—	1964	Glasgow Office closed.

Cont.

37

A 1819 – 0	Z 1844 – 5	D 1869 – 0	X 1894 – 5	V 1918 – 9	u 1943 – 4
B 1820 – 1	a 1845 – 6	Z 1870 – 1	Y 1895 – 6	W 1919 – 0	V 1944 – 5
C 1821 – 2	B 1846 – 7	A 1871 – 2	Z 1896 – 7	X 1920 – 1	W 1945 – 6
D 1822 – 3	C 1847 – 8	B 1872 – 3	A 1897 – 8	Y 1921 – 2	X 1946 – 7
E 1823 – 4	D 1848 – 9	C 1873 – 4	B 1898 – 9	Z 1922 – 3	y 1947 – 8
F 1824 – 5	E 1849 – 0	D 1874 – 5	C 1899 – 0	a 1923 – 4	Z 1948 – 9
G 1825 – 6	F 1850 – 1	E 1875 – 6	D 1900 – 1	b 1924 – 5	A 1949 – 50
H 1826 – 7	G 1851 – 2	F 1876 – 7	E 1901 – 2	c 1925 – 6	B 1950 – 1
I 1827 – 8	H 1852 – 3	G 1877 – 8	F 1902 – 3	d 1926 – 7	C 1951 – 2
J 1828 – 9	I 1853 – 4	H 1878 – 9	G 1903 – 4	e 1927 – 8	D 1952 – 3
K 1829 – 0	J 1854 – 5	I 1879 – 0	H 1904 – 5	f 1928 – 9	E 1953 – 4
L 1830 – 1	k 1855 – 6	J 1880 – 1	I 1905 – 6	g 1929 – 0	F 1954 – 5
M 1831 – 2	L 1856 – 7	K 1881 – 2	J 1906 – 7	h 1930 – 1	G 1955 – 6
N 1832 – 3	M 1857 – 8	L 1882 – 3	K 1907 – 8	i 1931 – 2	H 1956 – 7
O 1833 – 4	N 1858 – 9	M 1883 – 4	L 1908 – 9	j 1932 – 3	J 1957 – 8
P 1834 – 5	O 1859 – 0	N 1884 – 5	M 1909 – 0	k 1933 – 4	L 1958 – 9
Q 1835 – 6	P 1860 – 1	O 1885 – 6	N 1910 – 1	l 1934 – 5	M 1959 – 60
R 1836 – 7	Q 1861 – 2	P 1886 – 7	O 1911 – 2	m 1935 – 6	N 1960 – 1
S 1837 – 8	R 1862 – 3	Q 1887 – 8	P 1912 – 3	n 1936 – 7	O 1961 – 2
T 1838 – 9	S 1863 – 4	R 1888 – 9	Q 1913 – 4	o 1937 – 8	P 1962 – 3
U 1839 – 0	T 1864 – 5	S 1889 – 0	R 1914 – 5	p 1938 – 9	R 1963 – 4
V 1840 – 1	U 1865 – 6	T 1890 – 1	Since 1914-5	q 1939 – 0	Closed 1964
W 1841 – 2	V 1866 – 7	U 1891 – 2	S 1915 – 6	r 1940 – 1	
X 1842 – 3	W 1867 – 8	V 1892 – 3	T 1916 – 7	s 1941 – 2	
Y 1843 – 4	X 1868 – 9	W 1893 – 4	U 1917 – 8	t 1942 – 3	

Reigning Sovereign	Date of Accession	Date of Act, etc.	
Elizabeth II	—	1973	Hallmarking Act incorporated platinum; defined sponsors' marks; required dealers to display notices; defined what may be called gold, silver, and platinum in the course of trade or business; described what additions, alterations and repairs may be made without resubmission for Assay; and set up the British Hallmarking Council.

Cont.

DUBLIN DATE LETTERS

Letter	Year	Letter	Year	Letter	Year	Letter	Year	Letter	Year	Letter	Year
A	1638 – 9	o	1671 – 2	a	1720 – 1	I	1757 – 8	S	1790 – 1	C	1823 – 4
B	1639 – 0	p	1672 – 3	B	1721 – 2	K	1758 – 9	T	1791 – 2	D	1824 – 5
C	1640 – 1	q	1673 – 4	C	1722 – 3	L	1759 – 0	U	1792 – 3	E e	1825 – 6
D	1641 – 2	r	1674 – 5	D	1723 – 4	M	1760 – 1	W	1793 – 4	F	1826 – 7
E	1642 – 3	s	1675 – 6	E	1724 – 5	N	1761 – 2	X	1794 – 5	G	1827 – 8
F	1643 – 4	t	1676 – 7	F	1725 – 6	O	1762 – 3	Y	1795 – 6	H	1828 – 9
G	1644 – 5	u	1677 – 8	G	1726 – 7	P	1763 – 4	Z	1796 – 7	I	1829 – 0
H	1645 – 6	A	1678 – 9	H	1727 – 8	Q	1764 – 5	A	1797 – 8	K	1830 – 1
I	1646 – 7	B	1679 – 0	J	1728 – 9	R	1765 – 6	B	1798 – 9	L	1831 – 2
K	1647 – 8	C	1680 – 1	k	1729 – 0	S	1766 – 7	C	1799 – 0	M	1832 – 3
L	1648 – 9	D	1681 – 2	L	1730 – 1	T	1767 – 8	D	1800 – 1	N	1833 – 4
M	1649 – 0	E	1682 – 3	L	1731 – 2	U	1768 – 9	E	1801 – 2	O	1834 – 5
N	1650 – 1	F	1683 – 4	M	1732 – 3	W	1769 – 0	F	1802 – 3	P	1835 – 6
O	1651 – 2	G	1685 – 7	N	1733 – 4	X	1770 – 1	G	1803 – 4	Q	1836 – 7
P	1652 – 3	H	1688-93	O	1734 – 5	Y	1771 – 2	H	1804 – 5	R	1837 – 8
Q	1653 – 4	k	1694 – 5	P	1735 – 6	Z	1772 – 3	I	1805 – 6	S	1838 – 9
R	1654 – 5	L	1696 – 8	Q	1736 – 7	A	1773 – 4	K	1806 – 7	T	1839 – 0
S	1655 – 6	M	1699 – 0	R	1737 – 8	B	1774 – 5	L	1807 – 8	U	1840 – 1
T	1656 – 7	Ω	1700 – 1	S	1738 – 9	C	1775 – 6	M	1808 – 9	V	1841 – 2
U	1657 – 8	O	1701 – 2	T	1739 – 0	D	1776 – 7	N	1809 – 0	W	1842 – 3
a	1658 – 9	P	1702 – 3	U	1740 – 1	E	1777 – 8	O	1810 – 1	X	1843 – 4
b	1659 – 0	Q	1703 – 4	W W	1741 – 2	F	1778 – 9	P	1811 – 2	Y	1844 – 5
c	1660 – 1	R	1704 – 5	X	1743 – 4	G	1779 – 0	Q	1812 – 3	Z	1845 – 6
d	1661 – 2	S	1706 – 7	Y	1745 – 6	H	1780 – 1	R	1813 – 4	a	1846 – 7
e	1662 – 3	T	1708 – 9	Z	1746 – 7	I	1781 – 2	S	1814 – 5	b	1847 – 8
f	1663 – 4	U	1710 – 1	A	1747 – 8	K	1782 – 3	T	1815 – 6	c	1848 – 9
g	1664 – 5	W	1712 – 3	B	1748 – 9	L	1783 – 4	U	1816 – 7	d	1849 – 0
h	1665 – 6	X	1714 – 5	C	1749 – 0	M	1784 – 5	W	1817 – 8	e	1850 – 1
i	1666 – 7	Y	1715 – 6	D	1750 – 1	N	1785 – 6	X	1818 – 9	f f	1851 – 2
k	1667 – 8	Z	1716 – 7	E	1751 – 2	O	1786 – 7	Y	1819 – 0	g g	1852 – 3
l	1668 – 9	A	1717 – 8	F	1752 – 3	P	1787 – 8	Z	1820 – 1	h h	1853 – 4
m	1669 – 0	S	1718 – 9	G	1753 – 4	Q	1788 – 9	A	1821 – 2	j	1854 – 5
n	1670 – 1	T	1719 – 0	H	1754 – 5	R	1789 – 0	B	1822 – 3	k	1855 – 6

Letter	Year	Letter	Year	Letter	Year	Letter	Year	Letter	Year	Letter	Year
l	1856–7	I	1879–0	G	1902–3	B	1925–6	D	1945	Z	1967
m	1857–8	K	1880–1	H	1903–4	L	1926–7	E	1946	a	1969
n	1858–9	L	1881–2	I	1904–5	m	1927–8	F	1947	b	1968
o	1859–0	M	1882–3	k	1905–6	n	1928–9	G	1948	c	1970
p	1860–1	N	1883–4	L	1906–7	O	1929–0	H	1949	d	1971
Q	1861–2	O	1884–5	M	1907–8	P	1930–1	I	1950	e	1972
r	1862–3	P	1885–6	N	1908–9	From Jan 1st 1932 Assay Year and Calendar coincide		J	1951	f	1973
s	1863–4	Q	1886–7	O	1909–0			K	1952	S	1974
t	1864–5	R	1887–8	P	1910–1	P Used throughout 1931		L	1953	h	1975
u	1865–6	S	1888–9	Q	1911–2			M	1954	i	1976
v	1866–7	T	1889–0	R	1912–3	Q	1932	N	1955	L	1977
w	1867–8	U	1890–1	S	1913–4	R	1933	O	1956	m	1978
x	1868–9	V	1891–2	T	1914–5	S	1934	P	1957	n	1979
y	1869–0	W	1892–3	U	1915–6	C	1935	Q	1958	O	1980
z	1870–1	X	1893–4	A	1916–7	u	1936	R	1959	p	1981
A	1871–2	Y	1894–5	b	1917–8	v	1937	S	1960	R	1982
B	1872–3	Z	1895–6	C	1918–9	W	1938	T	1961	s	1983
C	1873–4	a	1896–7	D	1919–0	X	1939	U	1962	C	1984
D	1874–5	B	1897–8	e	1920–1	Y	1940	V	1963	u	1985
E	1875–6	C	1898–9	f	1921–2	Z	1941	W	1964	A	1986
F	1876–7	D	1899–0	S	1922–3	A	1942	X	1965	B	1987
G	1877–8	E	1900–1	h	1923–4	B	1943	Y	1966		
H	1878–9	J	1901–2	i	1924–5	C	1944				

Reigning Sovereign·	Date of Accession	Date of Act, etc.	
Elizabeth II	—	1975	Date letters brought into line by London, Birmingham, Sheffield and Edinburgh offices starting with A.
EEC Convention		1976	The Convention on the Control and Marketing of Precious Metals signed by Austria, Finland, Norway, Portugal, Sweden, Switzerland and the UK, accepting a Common Control Mark to free trading among them in precious metal articles.